TO JOE

'015

1 V

# THE LATEST MEWS

## LEARN TO SPEAK CAT 2

### By
### Anthony Smith

Souvenir Press

First published in Great Britain in 2014 by Souvenir Press Ltd
43 Great Russell Street, London WC1B 3PD

ISBN  9780285642867

Typeset by M Rules

Printed and bound in Croatia under supervision of MRM Graphics Ltd

Where cats first gained their fear of water

"Personally, I prefer your earlier work."

# ME~OWSE

"I'm having a working lunch."

"Don't feel too put out."

Small game hunter

Feline social gaffes

Mole in one

# HISSTRIONICS

"This is the *wrong* brand of cat food!"

If cats designed refrigerators

"Hello... I'd like to report a dangerous dog."

Goose bumps

"What do you mean, you don't have a leader?"

Mice hockey

"...and nap, two, three..."

Abusive tweets

When cats don't land on their feet

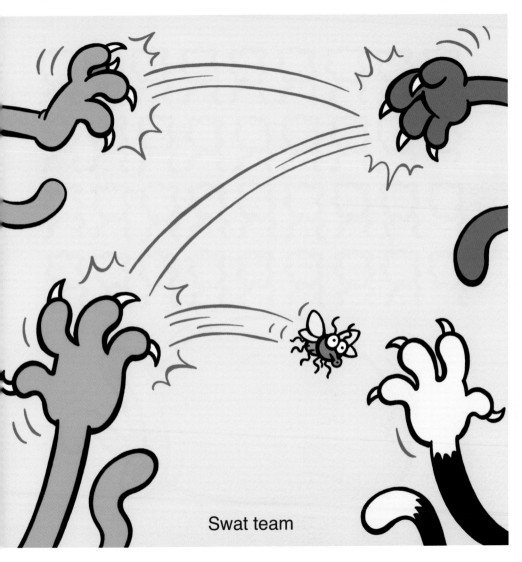

Swat team

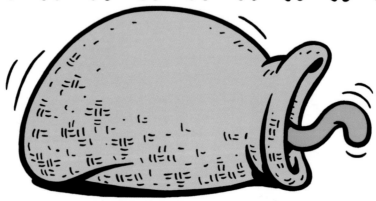

The joy of sacks

Cat nav

Gone mousing

Under mouse arrest

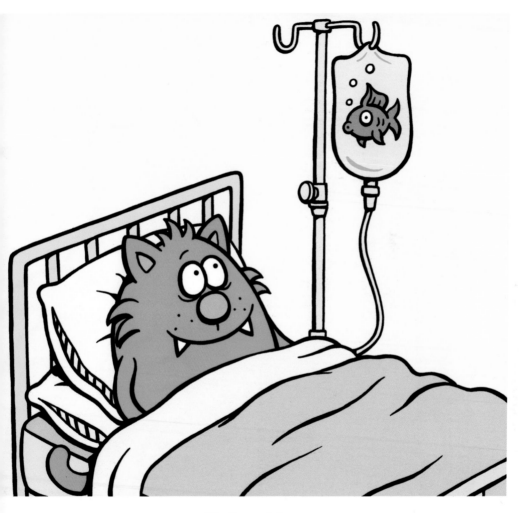

Feline drip

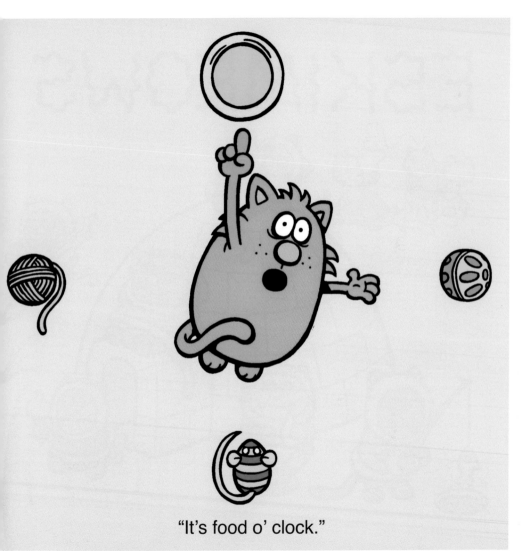

"It's food o' clock."

# ESKIMEOWS

Really cool cats

Cattoo

Why witches prefer black cats

"Trick or tuna?"

Games off the web

Big cat mystery solved

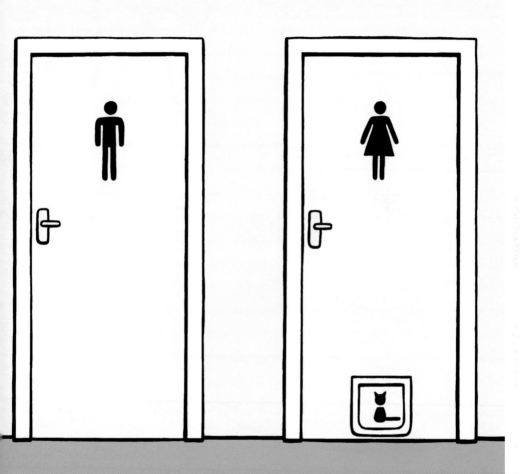

Puss in boots

"Play with your food!"

Cat basket ball

The hack-up

Meals on wheels

Trying to pull a fast one

Helveticat

Loitering within tent

Crazy cat lady search party

Bright idea

What bats think of cats

"You've got crow's feet."

Art that speaks to cats

How cats see birds

# NOSPURRATU

Unfed fiend

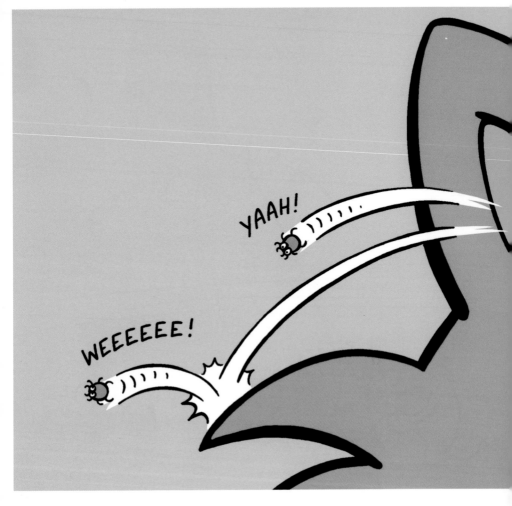

Lunaticks

"Does my bum look big is this collar?"

**KAT-POW**

"What the?!?..."

"I'm a big mouse... it's safe to come out."